D1325949

JN 03149789

Alfie's

Alphabet

Shirley Hughes

TED SMART

A TED SMART Publication 1999

3 5 7 9 10 8 6 4 2

First published 1997 by Red Fox, a division of Random House
This edition first published 1998 by The Bodley Head Children's Books
Random House, 20 Vauxhall Bridge Road, London SW1V 2SA
www.randomhouse.co.uk
A CIP catalogue record for this book is available from the British Library

Printed in Singapore
Colour Reproduction by Dot Gradations Ltd, U.K.

Random House UK Limited Reg. No. 954009

A a

A is for Alfie and his little sister, Annie Rose.

Bb

B is for
bedtime and
blanket.

C c

C is for Chessie, Alfie's black-and-white cat.

Dd

D is for drawing. Alfie is drawing
a picture of Annie Rose.

D is for door. (Be careful not to slam it!)

E is for elephant.
Alfie's elephant is nearly
as old as Alfie. He sleeps
in Alfie's bed every night.

F is for friends. Alfie's best friend is Bernard.

G is for Grandma. She can dance and sing and tell stories.

H h

H is for hat. This one's a bit too large for Alfie.

I i

I is for the insects Alfie loves to find under rocks.

J j J is for jacket.
In winter, Alfie
stays warm in his
red jacket.

K$_k$

K is for kitten.
This one is called
Boots.

L l

L is for lamb, Annie Rose's favourite toy.

M is for moon. A silver light, always changing shape. Magic moon.

M m

N is for neighbours. The MacNally family, who live across the street from Alfie, are very good neighbours indeed.

O o

O is for "Open the door, Alfie."

P p

P is for park and puddles!

Q is for questions. Alfie is very good at asking them. Luckily his friend Maureen is good at answers.

R is for reading. Maureen always reads Alfie
a story when she comes to baby-sit.

S s

S is for seaside, swimming, and sand castles.

T t

T is for tent,
teatime, and
teddies.

U u

U is for umbrella, which makes a good tent too, even when it's not raining.

V v

V is for visit, like when Grandma arrives
in her little red car.

W is for water (better outdoors than in!).

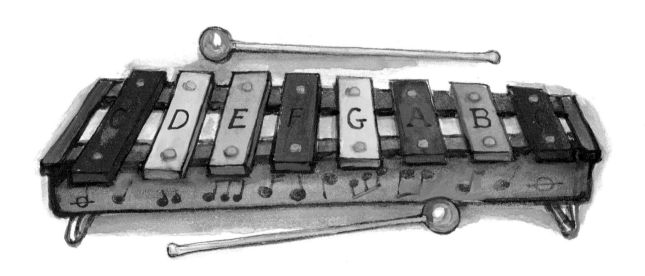

X is for Alfie's xylophone. Each bar has its own letter and makes a different sound when Alfie hits it.

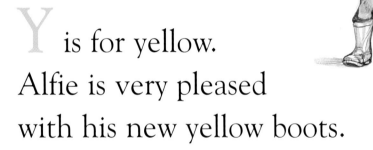

Y is for yellow.
Alfie is very pleased
with his new yellow boots.

Z_z

Z is for zip…
and this is the end of Alfie's ABC.